GW00362279

BURFORD
Historic Cotswold Town

Photographed by John Curtis

SALMON

INTRODUCTION

Burford hugs the slope of a Cotswold hill leading down to the aptly named River Windrush, where the sound of rushing water against a backdrop of rustling leaves has been heard by people who have lived and worked here for over 6,000 years. It is said that Queen Elizabeth I once stood on the medieval bridge across the river, gazing at the beauty of rural Oxfordshire with tears in her eyes. The view of Burford from the south is of unmeasurable beauty. The steep main street leads the eye down past splendid 17th and 18th century golden-stone houses, shops and inns, and the surrounding hills, fields and trees lend a perfect framework to an idyllic country scene.

The countryside provides perfect foraging for the renowned Burford Brown hen with its chocolate brown eggs, a bird that was originally introduced by local farmers during the early 1900s. Burford made its fortune through sheep and wool. An ancient merchant guild charter allowed independent markets to be held and tolls to be collected from those wishing to trade. It is thanks to this that Burford gained the status of 'town', despite a population of only about 1,000 souls.

William Morris, inspiration behind the Arts and Crafts movement, visited in 1876 and was appalled to find the local vicar scraping away medieval wall-paintings in the church. He protested at the disregard and the vicar's now famous reply "This church, sir, is mine, and if I choose to, I shall stand on my head in it", influenced the formation of the Society for the Protection of Ancient Buildings.

Burford

"Have nothing in your houses that you do not know to be useful, or believe to be beautiful", said William Morris who clearly appreciated the visual charm of this small town during visits in the 19th century. Historic visitors include Nell Gwynn who secretly met King Charles II here, resulting in a son who became Earl of Burford. Another claim to fame is the oldest pharmacy in England which was first established in Burford in 1734, known worldwide for its family-recipe handcream.

High Street, Burford

The wealth derived from the wool trade between the 14th and 17th centuries helped to create this 'street lost in time'. The unexpected harmony of the variety of architectural styles and periods contrasts perfectly with the ever-present surrounding hills.

The Tolsey, Burford

Wool merchants once held meetings and collected tolls at The Tolsey which stands appropriately at the corner of Sheep Street in the centre of town. The half-timbered early Tudor Court House has an open space beneath and today's visitors now enjoy the Tolsey Museum which occupies the first floor.

Former George Hotel, Burford
In common with many rural towns and villages, Burford once supported many more inns and pubs than exist today. The former George Hotel, with its courtyard to the rear, is a reminder of the town's former importance as a busy trading centre.

High Street, Burford
A blending of the Old English 'burh' meaning earthworks or defended settlement together with 'ford', a river crossing, gave the town its name. Burford is unusual in not having a distinct market place, but the particularly wide High Street fulfilled the function for the sale of local woollen cloth from as early as the 12th century. Medieval merchants or burghers developed long narrow burgage plots radiating away from the main street, and from these they were able to draw rent. Shops had workshops and stores behind the living quarters above. The resulting juxtaposition of buildings is a delight and gives the town its unique character.

St. John the Baptist's Church, Burford
The cathedral-like proportions of
St. John the Baptist's Church are
certainly impressive and this
magnificent building is one of the most
visited in England. It is described as the
'Queen of Oxfordshire, a paragon and
museum of the English Parish Church',
in Simon Jenkins' book: *England's
Thousand Best Churches*. Built in
Norman times and remodelled in the
15th century, a local gentleman named
Hercules Hastings was reputedly paid
£10 for making the original 'Old Turret
Clock' in 1685. The spacious
churchyard possesses a fine collection
of 'bale tombs' of the late 17th and
early 18th centuries – the tops
supposedly representing bales
of cloth.

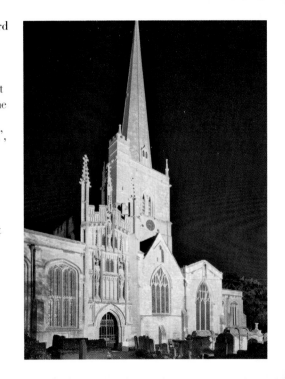

St. John the Baptist's Church, Burford

The church interior is overflowing with evidence of past riches, including an ornate tomb to Sir Lawrence Tanfield and his family. He was detested by many as Lord of the Manor because of his reputation for greed, corrupt practices and unwarranted interference. For 200 years after his death in 1628, local people burned his effigy in an annual celebration. Medieval wall-paintings still adorn some walls and also worthy of note is the Norman font adorned with 14th century carvings, sadly mutilated but still remarkably powerful. A further small mysterious carving positioned high on the side of the tower is at least of 12th century date, or possibly much earlier. The church was not always as peaceful as it is today. In 1649 Parliamentary troops mutinied at Salisbury and marched northwards, resting at Burford where Oliver Cromwell and Sir Thomas Fairfax caught up with them. After a fierce battle 340 'levellers', were imprisoned in the church. Three leaders were executed outside by the south wall, where bullet holes are still evident today.

Almshouses, Burford

The charming medieval almshouses on Church Green were licensed by Richard Neville 'The Kingmaker', Earl of Warwick and founded in 1457 by Henry Bishop of Burford. They were built for eight 'poor people of Burford' and the charming frontage remains largely intact, although the rest of the building was rebuilt in 1828. Pilgrims, nobles and merchants contributed 'alms', which also helped to repair the hospital chapel in 1305. The word 'alms' probably comes from eleemosyne, meaning pity or mercy in Ecclesiastical Greek.

Methodist Church, Burford

This grand Baroque town house of the early 18th century was stripped of its interior and converted into a Methodist church in 1849. From Burford it is just twenty miles to Oxford where John Wesley, the founder of Methodism, met regularly for Bible study and prayer.

Lamb Inn, Burford

The charming Lamb Inn could only be situated on Sheep Street, where this charming 15th century inn, restaurant and hotel was originally a row of weavers' cottages. Tradition has it that during the weekly sheep markets, shepherds looking for work used to gather outside this inn.

Sheep Street, Burford

There are numerous references in the town to the animal on which the fortunes of Burford were built, including a ram's head mounted on a limestone marker at the top of the hill. Leading off the High Street next to the Tolsey, Sheep Street was formerly the busy Cirencester to London road. It is now a quiet tree-lined street with mainly local stone-built houses and inns, many with characteristic steep gables and mullioned windows, including the handsome Bay Tree Hotel of 1649.

Riverside House, Burford

Situated near the bridge is Riverside House, home to Dr Cheatle during the Second World War. His father, Dr Thomas Cheatle, known for helping the poor, founded the Burford Cottage Hospital and designed surgical forceps known as 'Cheatle's forceps'.

Cotswolds Arms, Burford

Up to forty horse-drawn coaches a day once stopped in at Burford which was a major coaching halt with its many inns and free-flowing 'Burford bait'. The latter was said to loosen the wit before over imbuement resulted in drunkenness.

Port Mill, Burford

Several mills grew up around the river, and each developed its own specialisation. Some, it is said, made cloth that was dyed scarlet for uniforms for Oliver Cromwell's troops and red cloth could regularly be seen drying on hedges around the local countryside.

Westhall Hill Manor

This fine 17th century manor house stands in a hamlet of the same name and has wonderful views towards Burford and across the lush Windrush valley with its patchwork of fields divided by ancient drystone walls. The house has many period features including a fine carriageway arch.

River Windrush, Burford

No visit to Burford is complete
without a peaceful walk by the willow-
fringed banks of the river. The three-
arched pack-horse bridge is in constant
use and retains its medieval charm,
having very low sides in order to
accommodate the breadth of laden
'pack-horses' with their bulky loads
of wool and sheepskins.

The water divides under the bridge
where once the mill stream was vital
to the town's trades of wool and
leather tanning, rejoining the river
further to the east.

Taynton
Just a mile from Burford is this ancient settlement which can be traced back over 10,000 years. Cotswold stone has been quarried here since early medieval times, and was used in the Middle Ages for local churches and some of Oxford's colleges.

Windrush
The oldest date stone in this pretty quarrying village bears the inscription 1668 and the door to the Norman church is decorated by bird-like carvings known as 'beakheads'. To the south of Windrush lies an Iron Age hill-fort.

Westwell

The most westerly well in Oxfordshire gave this ancient village its Anglo-Saxon name 'Westwelle', recorded in the Domesday Book. Westwell Church was held by the Knights Hospitaller, a military order founded during the Crusades.

Little Barrington

The village is famous for being the home of fine stonemason Thomas Strong who helped build St. Paul's Cathedral. He left money in his will for the bridge, with instructions that it should be wide enough to allow men to carry a corpse across.

St. Oswald's Church, Widford

This tiny 11th century church in the Windrush Valley, with its original remnants of a dividing wall and rough font, is built on the foundations of a Roman villa. Other parts are 13th and 14th century, including several wall paintings. The raised terraces on the approach to St. Oswald's are the sole remains of the entire village of thirteen houses which was apparently abandoned in the Middle Ages during the Black Death. It was customary to ring the bell during times of trouble such as violent storms, approaching danger and death, believing that 'Silence is the Devil's medium'.

Swinbrook

The peaceful nature of this village heightens inside the church of St. Mary the Virgin where ornate 17th century monuments to the Fettiplace family adorn the chancel. The family were one of the largest landowners of the time, owning property in fifteen counties. The wall tombs each show three reclining Fettiplaces looking rather uncomfortable on their stone shelves. In the churchyard is the grave of Nancy Mitford, author of *Love in a Cold Climate*. Sister Jessica's autobiography tells of her Swinbrook upbringing, remembering how she accompanied 'Muv' to canvass for the Conservative Party during election time.

Minster Lovell Hall

Mystery and intrigue surround the ruins of this manor, which romantically sit beside the River Windrush and date from 1435. It was built by the Lovell family and the fate of the last Baron Lovell, who was found guilty of treason, has never been discovered.

Published by J. Salmon Ltd., Sevenoaks, Kent TN13 1BB. © 2008
Website: www.jsalmon.co.uk Telephone: 01732 452381. Email: enquiries@jsalmon.co.uk.

Design and photographs by John Curtis © John Curtis.
Printed in the EU.

ISBN 978-1-84640-129-1
Title page photograph: Bay Tree Hotel, Burford.   Front cover photograph: High Street, Burford.
Back cover photograph: Burford from the meadows.

Salmon Books

ENGLISH IMAGES SERIES

Photography by John Curtis

Titles available in this series

English Abbeys and Priories

English Gardens

English Country Towns

English Cottages

English Landscape Gardens

English Follies

English Villages

English Country Pubs

English Castles

English Cathedrals

English Country Churches

Jane Austen's England

Romantic England

Mysterious England